THE GOSPEL
ACCORDING TO
SCIENCE FICTION

THE GOSPEL ACCORDING TO SCIENCE FICTION

by
John Allan

Illustrated by
Rod Burke

PUBLISHED BY
QUILL PUBLICATIONS.

DISTRIBUTED BY
MOTT MEDIA.
POST OFFICE BOX 236
MILFORD MICHIGAN 48042.

Library of Congress Catalog Card No. 76-6920

NOV 22, 1976

ISBN 0-916608-02-6

Cover design and illustrations by Rod Burke

WHAT IS QUILL PUBLICATIONS?

A few years back a need was seen to help authors of merit find a means to bring their ideas to the attention of the public. Some of these authors had developed reputations based on previous writings, lectures and professional expertise, but many were new, young writers never having published, but with fresh ideas. Quill Publications was established to help these writers of merit reach the people that could best benefit from their knowledge and experience. Consequently, we have had enthusiastic support from educators, media people, artists and most important, you the reader. We are concerned that our publications are of high quality and readily available. At present we are attempting to find new works by good writers. These works may be fiction or non-fiction, textbooks or self help materials. It is from you the readers of our present publications that we are hoping to get these future books. We are interested in discussing with writers their ideas as they touch man's relationship to God, to himself, to his fellow man, and to his environment. If you feel you have something to contribute, we would like to hear from you.

TABLE OF CONTENTS

ACKNOWLEDGMENTS

I am not an astronomer, archaeologist, ancient historian, or astrophysicist. The only field in which I can lay claim to expert knowledge is Scottish literature; and so I am grateful for the painstaking help of others more knowledgeable than myself, in preparing this book for the press. All possible care has been taken to verify details and avoid factual error, but I will be grateful to hear from any reader who may spot in the text inaccuracies that have somehow slipped through. For errors I am totally responsible; for much help I am indebted to Colin Patterson, Dr. John Hutchison, Anthea White, Paul Allan, and most of all Mr. Richard Bell of the Bodleian Library. Finally, no one can write on this subject without incurring an immense debt to Barry Thiering and Edgar Castle's stimulating book, *Some Trust in Chariots!* I am no exception.

John Allan

INTRODUCTION

"The glorious Sun enchanted the Earth to splendour inspiring the Giants with the joy of life, the thrill of basking in the beauty of this wonderful world, living almost forever like the golden Sky Gods...children played and splashed in the sea pausing to stare wide-eyed as a gleaming vimana glided down towards the gilded towers of Lhasa, the Celestial City, whose translucent temples and flowery parks reminded the Venusians of their own fair planet." [1]

Science fiction? You might be excused for thinking so. In fact, says W. Raymond Drake, it's a sober and factual slice out of the history of this planet.

Were We "Created" By Astronauts?
Drake is one of a growing number of writers who have put forward, in the last few years, revolutionary new theories about the past history of the world.

Perhaps the best known is Erich von Däniken, who claims that we were originally "created" by astronauts; but there are many others. There is G.S. Hawkins, for example, who believes that Stonehenge is a monument of amazing precision, "a lonely monument to the scientific ability of prehistoric man."[2] There is Charles Berlitz, who asks in *Mysteries from Forgotten Worlds*, "Is it possible that there were other civilizations in the long history of Man that we know nothing of?" And the aged Guy Underwood claimed in 1968 that our "primitive" ancestors knew all about "geodetic law," a cosmic force which our so-called scientific mentality has ignored.[3]

Many of these radical new ideas involve space creatures. Von Däniken and his disciples believe that prehistoric art contains drawings of astronauts who visited this planet. Brinsley le Poer Trench, in a series of books, develops a theory about friendly Sky People who want to help us, and who are opposed by "the entities which inhabit the auric envelope (or astral area) of this planet." There is an ever-increasing public interest in flying saucers; a marketing firm called Paradise International, who developed a Flying Saucer Detector capable of reacting to hovering spacecraft in a millionth of a second, have now had to stop work on other products due to the avalanche of orders. Says company spokesman Paul Hoffman, "We've been selling the detector for five years now, but I've never seen the demands for it like this before."

Theories about UFOs multiply every minute. Brad Steiger and Joan Whritenour suggest in one book, *Flying Saucers are Hostile*, that "someone up there may not like us." In other books they have different theories:

"What if they don't come from outer space?"
"Is it possible the flying saucers are being manned by an ancient race from earth?"

"Do members of some ancient race walk among us...?"

Brian Aldiss, the most authoritative historian of science fiction, records that "the last few years bear testimony to the enormous diversity of science fiction— so great that one wing does not recognize the other as the same creature.

"My belief is that this diversification will increase, thus merging on the one side with comic books, the flickerings of television, and Dayglo Middle Earth posters; and on the other side with the sort of literature-of-extremity practiced by such very individual men as Samuel Beckett, William Burroughs, Lawrence Burrell, Anthony Burgess, *et al.*" [4]

The Influence of Science Fiction

Science fiction is becoming an important mythological influence on western culture. The diversification which Aldiss outlines explains why (for example) Stanley Kubrick can refer to *2001: A Space Odyssey* as a kind of religious experience. Science fiction started to shape and condition our thinking. Kubrick claimed that the idea of a supernatural God should give way to the concept of "gods" who are simply other races more advanced than ours.

"The important thing is that all the standard attributes assigned to God in our history could equally well be the characteristics of biological entities who billions of years ago were at a stage of development similar to man's own and developed into something as remote from man as man is remote from the primordial ooze from which he first emerged." [5]

The emphasis is on understanding mysterious, occult, or religious experience in *scientific* terms. A new book on astrology, for example, is recommended to the public in a way significantly different from the old make-astrology-work-for-you, discover-your-fate-from-the-stars line which used to be the main selling points:

"As man hurtles headlong through the Aquarian Age, he seeks a greater understanding through the physical and occult sciences of the universe he occupies... [This book] creates a deeper awareness of our own power and the reality we live in." [6]

Science, religions, the occult teachings of the past... the boundaries are becoming blurred. It is no coincidence that 1973 saw the publication of both Dr. Lyall Watson's *Supernature*, and the massive paperback edition of Colin Wilson's *The Occult*. Watson is a scientist who is interested in extending science into occult realms. Colin Wilson is a novelist whose interest in occult knowledge has grown out of scepticism over the last few years. "Magic was not the 'science' of the past. It is the science of the future. I believe that the human mind has reached a point in evolution where it is about to develop new powers—powers that would once have been considered magical."

Another feature of 1973 was the sudden discovery by hordes of precocious little boys that they had the strange ability to stop watches by thought, and bend spoons by stroking. This followed the TV appearances of Uri Geller, a young Israeli wonder-worker whose story has now been written by his friend and adviser Puharich. The book explains Uri's powers in a typically "sf" way: in charge of creation are a bunch of mysterious figures called The Nine, and the controllers of the universe are subservient to them. Between the controllers and the planetary civilizations, there are "messengers" who visit various people on each planet. Uri's powers are given to him by the "messengers" who have singled him out to receive their visits. Puharich comments:

"I had suspected for a long time from my researchers that man has been in communication with beings not of this earth for thousands of years.... With the publication of this book... many of the cosmic secrets are now declassified." [7]

Another ESP entertainer, George Kreskin, is extremely scornful of Uri's space stories. But he too declares, "I think the human mind awaits many new and startling uses." [8] Even the materialistic Soviet Union is reputed to be researching into telepathy and shadowy mental powers. And Dennis Bardens is able to begin *Mysterious Worlds* by claiming, "In recent years psychical phenomena and science have impinged increasingly upon each other... such matters... are no longer the domain of the superstitious, the credulous, the fearful or the merely romantic."

16 The Gospel According to Science Fiction

Science Fiction Gospels

Out of it all has come what I have christened The Gospel According to Science Fiction—the belief, in one shape or another, that the secrets of the past and the prospects of the future can be ascertained by a new "scientific" look at puzzling mysteries and what we know about flying saucers. In the next few chapters I shall be examining some of the main preachers of this Gospel; and deciding whether or not their revolutionary new ideas contribute anything to our knowledge of ourselves. My survey will, I hope, be as open-minded as possible; it may be amusing, for I believe that the unexplained mysteries of the world are not half so strange as most of the things that have been written about them; and then in the last chapter I want to suggest a sure-fire way of knowing *for certain* which theories are true, and which are a load of...science fiction.

Notes to Introduction

1. W. Raymond Drake, *Gods and Spacemen in the Ancient East* (1973), page 68.
2. G.S. Hawkins, *Beyond Stonehenge* (1973), page 1. See also Hawkins and J.B. White, *Stonehenge Decoded.*
3. Guy Underwood, *The Pattern of the Past* (1968).
4. B.W. Aldiss, *Billion Dollar Spree* (1973), page 319.
5. Kubrick interviewed by *Playboy* in 1968. Reprinted in J. Agel ed., *The Making of Kubrick's 2001* (New York, 1970), pages 331-2.
6. Alan Oken, *As Above, So Below* (New York, 1973).
7. A. Puharich, *Uri* (1973).
8. G. Kreskin, *The Amazing World of Kreskin* (1974).

CHAPTER I

GOD WORE
A SPACE SUIT

CHAPTER I

GOD WORE A SPACESUIT

What About Chariots of the Gods?
By far the most popular of the God-was-an-astronaut theorists is Erich von Däniken. A Swiss hotel-keeper with no scientific education, but with convictions for embezzlement, fraud and forgery, may not sound likely material for a best-selling author; but with 25 million readers worldwide, a film, an LP record and various successful lecture tours to his credit, von Däniken has to be taken seriously.

His first book, *Chariots of the Gods?*, has been on sale in England since 1969; and yet still, as I write this, one of the main bookshops in Oxford is devoting its front window to a display of copies. It's impossible to read his books in the City Library; they are perpetually out on loan. And in Australia, such has been the massive wave of public interest in him that the newspapers have labelled it "Danikenitis." Is it what the name suggests—an impulsive, irrational epidemic?

Or are there good reasons for the conversion of so many people to his theories?

Some of the evidence he puts forward is startling enough. Maps, he says, were found in the Topkapi Palace at the start of the 18th century, which had

belonged to a Turkish admiral, Piri Re'is. When examined by modern scholars, they were found to give absolutely accurate outlines of the coasts of North and South America, as well as the Antarctic. Mountain ranges, rivers and islands were drawn with extreme accuracy. Even more amazing, mountain ranges were shown in the Antarctic which Piri couldn't have known—they've been buried in ice for centuries, and were first discovered, with echo-sounding equipment, in 1952. Who drew Piri's maps?

A piece of cloth was discovered at Helwan, centuries old, which would apparently require a special modern fabric factory to manufacture. Who made it?

An island in the Nile was called Elephantinos because in shape it was like an elephant. A fact you'd only notice *from the air*—so who went up to find that out?

An Amazing Theory About Man's Origin
From details like that, Erich von Däniken has constructed an amazing theory about the origins of humanity. In the unknown past, he says, there was a battle in the depths of the galaxy between two space peoples like us. The losers escaped in a spaceship to earth, and built tunnel systems underground to avoid detection by their pursuers. Eventually they emerged from the tunnels and began to create human life *"in their own image* from already existing monkeys." After that they decided that the evolutionary process was too slow, and in impatience wiped out "those who did not follow the biological laws laid down"[1] (a cryptic phrase I don't pretend to understand). Subsequently men began to dig underground hideouts themselves, for fear of "divine judgment." Eventually the astronauts took off for fresh fields and pastures new, but still they're watching us, curious about the results of their experiment.

God Wore a Space Suit 23

"Powerful stuff," commented the *Daily Mail*, "which, no matter how one tries, cannot be discarded as crackpot theories." Scientists have disagreed. "I am at a loss to see it as a serious scientific exercise," remarked P.J. Grouse, Senior Lecturer in Computer Studies at the University of New South Wales. Experts in other fields have been equally dismissive. "From the point of view of the Mesopotamian evidence," claimed Dr. N.K. Weeks, a specialist in ancient history, "this book is so full of error, mis-statement and untruth as to be worthless." And E.C.B. Maclaurin, Head of the Department of Semitic Studies at Sidney, agrees, "Von Daniken's book is superficially plausible but cannot stand up to examination."[2]

Von Däniken retaliates by suggesting that his critics have blinkered minds. They have an interest in dismissing his arguments, because it would be too challenging to take them seriously. Who is right?

The "Space Slips" of Von Däniken
"Erich von Däniken has the spontaneity of the enthusiast," claims his admirer, Wilhelm Roggersdorf. "He hops on planes to clear up his theories the way we catch a bus." If this is so, one wonders why his checking of the most obvious details is so slipshod. "Without actually consulting Exodus, I seem to re-member...."[3] And it's as well he *didn't* consult Exodus; he wouldn't have found the details he "seems to remember." As it is, he makes five simple mistakes in two pages. There's no mention in Exodus of gold plates; of slashing sparks; of alloys used on construc-ting the ark . . . and so on. Slips like this don't fill one with confidence. It is also disconcerting that on the first page of his first book he calls the earth a star (which it isn't), and then attempts to calculate the number of miles in a light year — which simple calculation[4] he fouls up by a factor of 60....

The photographs of the Plain of Nazca look very impressive. Miles and miles of strange markings, he cries, on the surface of the plain — what could these be but runways for aircraft? What else indeed — until you realize that the surface is not rock, but *soil* — and the

first blast of aircraft slipstream would blow the "air-field" away! Surely he should have known this?

Then there's his odd, erudite way of discounting the "fairy tales" he was told as a child:

"Today I know that there is no mention of Lucifer in the Old Testament. It would be impossible, anyway, for the legendary figure of Moses, in whom the authors of the Old Testament are subsumed, is supposed to have lived about 1225 BC, but Lucifer comes from Latin and that language is dated to 240 at the earliest." [5]

How impressive it sounds — and how irrelevant. Thirty seconds with a concordance would have shown him that Isaiah (much later than Moses!) *does* mention Lucifer; and half an ounce of common sense would have led him to reflect that "Lucifer" was only the Latin translation of the real Hebrew name used by Isaiah.

This slipshod approach to matters of fact can help him to make a thing sound mysterious when it isn't. Take for example the facts we began with. The Piri Re'is map is not at all wonderful; we know who made it — Piri claimed he had made it himself, based on older charts including some deriving from the work of Columbus. And as you'd expect, the map reflects the knowledge of sailors who had explored as far south as the Amazon but had gone no further (Magellan would be the first to do that, six years after Piri drew his map). It is *not* accurate south of the Amazon, and does not show inland details. Antarctica is not shown, but Japan is... where Cuba ought to be.

The Helwan cloth? Spinning and weaving had been known for 2000 years or more at that time, and, not surprisingly, some people were rather good at it! The modern fabric factory is pure imagination.

As for Elephantinos, it may look like an elephant *now,* but its shape has certainly changed over the centuries! In fact (as von Däniken should know!) the Greek word *elephantinos* means "ivory" not "like an elephant"—and the island was quite simply the site of an ivory market.

God Wore a Space Suit 29

"And in places," complains Colin Wilson, "he displays a lack of logic that amounts almost to imbecility. Describing a skeleton carved out of stone which he located in an underground chamber, he says, 'I counted ten pairs of ribs, all anatomically accurate. Were there anatomists who dissected bodies for the prehistoric sculptor? As we know, Wilhelm Conrad Röntgen did not discover the new kind of rays he called X-rays until 1895!' The mind boggles at the mad illogicality: the idea that a sculptor would need X-rays to see a skeleton, when every graveyard must have been full of them. It is equally puzzling how his publishers allowed him to put such an absurdity into print." [6]

Many of his grand statements are so vague as to be meaningless. "Chariots of light, wheels and smoke were spoken of as magnificent apparitions as early as and in connection with Adam and Eve." [7] As early as Adam and Eve!? But this kind of imprecision is his trademark. He says that all the cuneiform texts from Ur are exciting documents telling about gods. Well, here's a sample:

"Come now, Cleaner, let me give you an order — clean my suit. Don't lay aside the order I give you."

"Actually," he remarks, "the ancient gods were always telling us that we were deaf and blind, but that one day we should know the 'truth'." [8] *Which* ancient gods? The statement is too wide to mean anything at all.

Can We Check the Truth of the Theories
But imprecision is even more crucial when it means that no one can check the truth of what he says. He tells an odd story about graves discovered in Northern China by archaeologist Chi Pu Tei. Mysterious inscrip-

tions found there were deciphered by Chinese scientist Tsum Um Nui, and their story was so shattering that the Peking Academy of Prehistory banned publication of it. The details were given to von Däniken by Soviet writer Alexandr Kasantsev.

Gordon Creighton, a journalist interested in flying saucers, decided to investigate the truth. He approached Chinese professors and scientific academies with no success, and Kazantsev wrote to say that he didn't tell von Däniken the story—von Däniken had told it to him! Finally, Creighton found that he couldn't even identify the Chinese "experts" named by von Däniken.

"*Tsum, Um* and *Nui* are not monosyllables used in the transliteration of the standard spoken Chinese.... It could possibly be derived from an obscure and remote dialect, but the person of Tsum Um Nui has remained unidentifiable. The same is true for the alleged archaeologist discoverer of the grave site, Chi Pu Tei, because *Tei* is an unrecognizable corruption, not used with the first part of the man's name, Chi Pu." [9]

What really happened? The more we probe into the facts, the more they seem to recede.

Von Däniken is Just Plain Wrong

On top of slipshod checking, mystification, loose statements, sometimes von Däniken is just plain *wrong* in what he wrote. Enoch did not disappear in a chariot of fire. The Olmec stone heads are not too heavy to transport (one was recently on display at the New York Metropolitan Museum of Art, thousands of miles away). It would not take 664 years to build the Great Pyramid. It would not take hundreds of thousands of laborers to move the stone blocks. The total construction would not weigh 31,200,000 tons. Ropes and wood were not unavailable to the builders—you can see a fair amount of the "non-existent" rope in the Cairo museum, and ancient Egypt imported wood from at least nine countries. The area of the base divided by the height doesn't give pi if you use cubits or feet and inches; your unit has to be 128.77 cubits, which isn't anybody's unit of measurement—except, seemingly, von Däniken's.

Features which he quotes from the Gilgamesh Epic just aren't there. . . . The Sumerians did *not* have highly developed astronomy (unless he means that they left a list of 25 stars behind!). And so the list could be multiplied.

The Fertile Imagination of Von Däniken
But what von Däniken lacks in factuality he makes up for in imagination. *Gold of the Gods*, also by von Däniken, contains an illustration of an amulet, on which is drawn the picture of a man standing above a circle which is crossed by various lines. "How," demanded von Däniken in triumph, "did Stone Age men know that the earth was round?"[10] He never doubts for a moment that this crudely-drawn, squashed-looking circle is meant to depict the earth, or that the man is meant to be standing on it.

"Nobody seems to suggest," wails Peter Lewis, "except me, that these weird depictions by cavemen look like they do because the artists were *not very good* at drawing, or were *not trying* to be realistic."[11]

Von Däniken's favorite illustration of his theory is a sarcophagus relief from Palenque, which he says shows an astronaut blasting off in his rocket. There are even "flames" at the bottom of the picture. He omits to explain that there's a skull beneath the pilot seat, not to mention a bird perched on the nosecone; and that the astronaut is sticking his head outside the rocket. Gordon Whittaker comments ironically:

God Wore a Space Suit 33

"One has to hand it to von Daniken for not being fooled by the arrogant members of the Establishment who say that the relief only shows a Maya dignitary on a throne above the skull of the Lord of the Earth, and that the dignitary is about to pluck a fruit from the Tree of Life, on top of which is a sacred bird representing the zenith direction." [12]

Certainly—I think they would have fooled me.

Can it be a coincidence, asks von Däniken portentously, that the Quiché *Popol Vuh* displays extensive similarity to the Old Testament? Having now read the Popol Vuh, I'm at a loss to find any similarity at all. In fact von Daniken lists about the only four features the two books have in common:

1. The whole earth being "of one language and of one speech."

2. Men in a fiery furnace (but there's no Son of God there in the Popol Vuh, and the men aren't thrown in).

3. Mention of a covenant in both books—but with a totally different significance in the two cases.

4. The crossing of seas dryshod in both books (but by different methods: in Exodus a strong wind parts the waves; in the Popol Vuh "round stones rose from the sand and they walked across on the rows of stones").

Once again, his fertile imagination has simply run away with him. The differences between the Hebrews and the Quiché (who probably had ten pairs of "major gods," one for each of the twenty months in their *may q'ih* cycle) are far more striking than any supposed connections.

The way he argues allows his imagination total freedom. He just cannot lose. Anything impressive in Maya civilization can be ascribed to astronauts; anything less so (human sacrifices, for instance; worshippers offering blood from their ears and tongue to the gods; artificial deformation of the head; the severe limitations of their architecture, due to failure to develop the true arch) can be attributed to the gradual loss of the knowledge that the astronauts handed down!

God Wore a Space Suit 35

The Theories Raise Important Questions

His theories raise more questions than they answer (if the Israelites used a sound wave "death trumpet" at Jericho why didn't it work till the seventh day they used it?) yet he never admits that there are any improbabilities inherent in his ideas. But assume for a moment that his claims are correct. Why then did the astronauts spread their efforts around the globe, rather than concentrating on one place and one manageable civilization? They seem to have made a point of heading for the most inconvenient places to carry on their "experiment." And how do we explain the colossal differences between different nations' accounts of creation, or between different religions? Why is the stern, moral monotheism of the Hebrews so different from the creed of most of the nations they came into contact with? Why have we found no artifacts from space in the course of our archaeological investigations? *Our* rubbish will be around for centuries to show what our culture was like; wouldn't one expect a highly-developed space civilization to leave at least some traces?

The questions mount up and will not be answered. If we were "created" by astronaut scientists, who made the astronaut scientists? Did *they* have to be created by interplanetary visitors too—or is it possible that their advanced civilization arose quite naturally without any outside help? And if *their* civilization could come about without astronaut help...couldn't ours have done so too?

Von Däniken criticizes scientists as cowards because they will not accept his ideas. He declares, "I am still too young to be able to resign myself. I believe in the disturbing power of ideas that cannot be hushed up." But he doesn't see that his ideas are of no use to science at the moment, because they can't be proved or disproved! Scientists only make advances when they're

God Wore a Space Suit 37

able to test out the ideas which come to them. That car engines are really operated by little green men who live inside, but disappear as soon as you open the hood, is an interesting idea—but you can't prove it one way or the other. That petrol ignited in a closed chamber will provide energy enough to make the wheels go round, is an idea we *can* test out, and it's led to the construction of automobiles!

Von Däniken assumes that if we met up again with our spacemen "creators," we would automatically benefit from watching their superior technology in action. But it's a well-known sociological fact that, when an inferior culture meets up with a superior one, the inferior culture becomes demoralized and may even lose knowledge it already possesses! James Burke pointed out in a recent "Burke Special" that if we contacted more advanced forms of life, we would no longer have the stimulating challenge of finding things out for ourselves—we would be fed what we needed to know like animals.

Bruno Ghibaudi actually believes that flying saucers are deliberately *avoiding* us so as not to hinder our development. "Do not let us forget that between their science and ours there is a gap of thousands of years....How could such an encounter be permitted? At an inner level, we should quite certainly be severely shaken as a result." [13] John Michell, another God-was-an-astronaut theorist, agrees. "In our present state of unpreparedness the sudden forcible introduction of such an idea into our conscious minds would be calamitous." [14]

And so Erich von Däniken has erected a theory that cannot be proved, but has several grave objections against it, on the foundation of slipshod reasoning and dubious facts. The staggering thing is not that scientists have shown him so little respect. The staggering thing is that he should have sold so many books, and confused so many people!

Notes to Chapter I

1. *Gold of the Gods* (1973), tr. M. Heron, page 46.
2. See their articles in B. Thiering and E. Castle, eds., *Some Trust in Chariots!* (Folkestone, 1973).
3. *Chariots of the Gods?* page 58.
4. Later editions corrected.
5. *Gold of the Gods*, page 46.
6. C. Wilson, *Strange Powers* (1973), page 16.
7. *Chariots of the Gods?* page 60.
8. *Return to the Stars*, page 177.
9. *Faith and Fortune 2* (1974), page 39.
10. *Gold of the Gods,* page 11.
11. Peter Lewis in the *Daily Mail*, June 20, 1974.
12. In Thiering and Castle, op cit, page 60.
13. Quoted by G.W. Creighton, in *Flying Saucer Review*, Vol. 9, No. 3 (1963), pages 18-20.
14. John Michell, *Flying Saucer Vision* (1967), page 15.

CHAPTER II
THE BIBLE
TELLS ME SO

CHAPTER II

THE BIBLE TELLS ME SO

"Space gods made me, this I know,
For the Bible tells me so...."

Bible-ized Theories of Astronaut Gods
Some of von Däniken's weakest evidence is drawn
from the Bible. "I do not think von Däniken knows the
Bible very well," admits his Presbyterian admirer, Dr.
Barry Downing. "I do not recommend von Däniken as a
careful biblical scholar, nor as a theologian...."[1]
However, various other writers have tried to work out a
modified theory by examining the Bible more carefully;
and here we shall look at three of them.

W. Raymond Drake and Astronaut Legends
W. Raymond Drake is not very interested in sarco-
phagi, inscriptions and cave drawings. His primary
interest is in *legends*—scores of which he quotes at
length in his books, *Gods and Spacemen in the Ancient
East* and *Gods and Spacemen in the Ancient West*. His

basic idea is that all ancient peoples preserve legends of supermen from the stars who once ruled and guided earth, and that by comparing the different accounts we can arrive at what really happened.

In the Golden Age, when the Giants of Earth were ruled by Saturnians, evil invaders from Jupiter arrived to provoke the Giants into revolt. War was waged in earth and sky, using nuclear weapons and laser rays, and the ravaging effects can still be seen today. Later, the Lords of Sirius (who direct· the destinies of this planet) sent an asteroid hurtling at Earth "in divine retribution," and to start off a new "world-age." The Golden Age civilization was wrecked, and only a few people survived. They implored the Gods to help Earth again; and a few Extra-terrestrials descended in their ships of light to teach man civilization. The rest is history.

We could ask why there are absolutely no relics of this supertechnological age to be found anywhere; or why the Extra-terrestrial teaching program achieved such unsatisfactory, fragmentary results. Be that as it may, Drake links this scheme to a kind of science-fiction Hinduism. "The human soul evolves by metempsychosis, reincarnating life after life ascending to perfection in God.... The Earth is a training-school to which the soul returns to learn its lessons, then is reborn on a more highly developed planet, ascending through a chain of worlds assimilating experience."[2]

"Useful" Distinctions
And so he can make a distinction—very useful for his purposes!—between God, the Absolute, and gods, spacemen with limited super-powers. Tricky passages in world literature can be interpreted either way. Thus there's no real contradiction between legends that speak of one god, and legends that insist on several; between religions that treat God as a person, and

religions that think of him as an impersonal force. God the Absolute is unique and impersonal; but the gods (i.e., space visitors) are personal and many! "Jehovah Himself was probably a Spaceman, but the esoteric teachings of Judaism acknowledge the Supreme Essence of God, the Creator" (page 169).

Synthesis, then, is vital. Only by sticking myths together do you arrive at the whole truth. The trouble is that his reconstruction looks *nothing like* the teaching of any one individual account.

Much of his argument is wrong-headed. It's not just that he gets his facts wrong (Virgil did not teach reincarnation, the Dead Sea Scrolls do nothing to cast doubt on Christianity, the Bible is not mistaken about Dairus' conquest of Babylon, Mariolatry is not the "purest esoteric form" of Christianity but an extremely late development). It isn't just that he makes statements so sweeping that they couldn't possibly be true ("All religions teach of the Angels of Light warring against the powers of darkness for possession of Man's soul." page 10). More importantly, he has to alter his texts, cut out bits and stitch them together again, in order to fit them into his scheme. "This confused story is probably some race-memory of. . . ." Biblical events "may be a version of," "may represent," "may be a garbled memory of," something quite different. It's not very scientific to build up a theory on the basis of certain facts—and then alter the facts, because they don't quite suit the theory.

Pick and Choose What Fits Your Theory.
There is something contradictory about the man who draws evidence for his theory from the Book of Exodus, then goes on to say, "The account of the Exodus seems not to be real history but magic and myth. . . . The book of Exodus is not a factual, critical record of events" (page 158).

So he takes from legends what suits his theory, and discards the rest. He tells the Chinese tale about Heng-O, who ate a magic pill and flew off to the moon, which she found to be covered in cinnamon trees. Later her husband Tzu-yu ate a magic cake and then rode off on the back of an enchanted bird to the sun. Remembering his wife, he sped down a beam of light to the moon, and built her a palace of cinnamon trees to cheer her up. And Drake's comment? "This legend may perpetuate most ancient teachings that both sun and moon were inhabited" (page 82). What, we cry, about the cinnamon trees, magic food, enchanted birds and beams of light? How on earth do they fit in?

Although he has no faith in the Bible's accuracy, he does trust lesser-known sources. The implication obviously is that the more esoteric a document, the more we can trust it. Unfortunately, the Genesis Apocryphon (which he uses to correct the biblical account) is worthless as prehistory; it was produced by an imaginative group of speculative thinkers in the 1st or 2nd century BC. The Talmud is a commentary on the Old Testament, and was never thought to carry the same authority.

And the important question, which he never faces, is: how far can you *trust* "garbled race-memories and folk-lore" which "imagined the Spacemen to be Gods with superhuman powers"? If the legends are so fragmentary, so wrongly conceived and so confused— how does W. Raymond Drake know that he isn't extracting from them exactly what he intended to find?

Barry Downing and the Scientific "Miracles"
Barry Downing's sermons must be interesting. For the Flying Saucer theorist who goes the opposite way from Drake, and tries to take the Bible more seriously as it stands, is a young clergyman. Rev. Dr. Barry

Downing is Pastor of Northminster Presbyterian Church, New York City, and holds a physics degree from Hartwick College, Oneonta, New York. Not surprisingly, he is unhappy with von Däniken's haphazard treatment of the Bible, and has his own theory to suggest.

"It is very clear from the Exodus story," he claims, "that if the Hebrew people were in contact with what von Däniken calls "ancient astronauts" then the Jewish religion is not an accidental misinterpretation of "gods in the sky" by the Jews, but rather these "gods" or "angels" have given the Jews a religion in the laboratory of the wilderness *on purpose!*" [3]

Modern theologians, he says, find miracles quite incredible, and so have felt the need to "demythologize" the Scriptures, explaining away miraculous events. "The Biblical material in many ways seems scientifically impossible, and because of this the Biblical idea of God seems impossible—God must be dead" (pages 21-22).

Ah, but if the miracles can be explained scientifically —if the biblical religion was a "package" delivered by astronauts—then we can accept the Bible stories once again! And, he says, only one question will remain to be answered: is Christianity a kind of interplanetary hoax, invented by practical jokers in space-suits to keep us guessing, or were these astronauts acting at God's command?

His difficulties begin, though, when he tries to separate scientific facts from religious "myth." "We have to admit immediately that there is much historical evidence to support the view that much of the Biblical material is mythological. . . . Everyone seems to agree that Jesus really—literally—was crucified. But when we read that Thomas sought to touch the wounds in the hands of the risen Christ,[4] our scientific imagination is stretched, and we then suggest that this report has a mythological origin'' (pages 24-25).

Biblical Fact and Fancy

How then do we tell the difference between "Biblical fact and fancy"? The best Downing can suggest is: "to investigate on one hand to what extent the materials involved seem to represent an interpretation of a particular experience, and on the other hand what materials comprise *description*, or reporting of empirical data."

Now that's not very satisfactory, because it means you can read the Bible in whatever way you wish. If a certain detail fits in with your astronaut theory, you call it "description"; if it *doesn't* fit, it becomes a "religious interpretation." "We may want to accept both the 'data' and the conclusion, or we may want to accept only the data. In the case of the Red Sea incident, I accepted the data that an east wind was blowing, but I did not accept the Biblical conclusion that the wind *caused* the water to part" (page 122). It is not so easy as Downing thinks to separate "sense data" from "interpretation."

How does he know what UFOs can do? His argument is that miracles were caused, not by scientific means which we now understand, but by scientific means which we still *don't!* Thus he makes as big an act of faith to believe in Astronauts, as traditional Christians make to believe in God.

But the most serious objection is simply this: why do we *need* his kind of explanation? Are miracles so incredible? "I once heard a theological professor raise the following rhetorical question in his class: 'No one today believes in the Ascension, does he?'" (page 21). Well, does that prove anything, I wonder, except the arrogant prejudice of the professor concerned? Whatever some theologians believe, many scientists—like

Professor Malcolm Jeeves—find nothing incredible in the idea of miracles:

"The Christian viewpoint, we maintain, is more open-minded, in that in the first place it agrees that it is perfectly legitimate to assume uniformity in nature, but at the same time it is willing to entertain the possibility of miracle, if there are found to be good historical grounds for doing so. In other words, our conception of natural laws accepts the fact that they are based on a comparatively small number of observations or experiments, and that they must always remain subservient to, rather than normative over, any further observations." [5]

A Shaky Reading of the Bible

Barry Downing uses a shaky reading of the Bible to justify an unnecessary argument containing many improbabilities when worked out in full. His suggestion of an anti-G beam at the crossing of the Red Sea may be clever; his suggestion that the baptized Jesus was taken off in a space-craft *isn't*. And he leaves us asking three questions:

1. If the whole business is just an elaborate game which is being played by more advanced beings, why did they bother? They've taken a terrific amount of trouble over it—even sending one of their number to be crucified.

2. If God is really behind it all, why postulate these intermediaries? It is no less "scientific" to believe in miracles than it is to believe in spacemen with unimagined powers!

3. Do we have to judge the Christian faith by its *probability*? Are we wrestling in the dark with a few cryptic ancient documents, trying to make sense of

what did and didn't happen—or is there a way of being *certain* whether Christianity is true or false?

But we shall look more closely at this third question in a moment!

R.L. Dione and the "Supertechnological" God

If Barry Downing's astronauts seem to have no convincing motives, R.L. Dione, a middle-aged schoolteacher, who was once a paratrooper and a boxer, thinks he can suggest some. The Bible, he says, must be taken "literally," except that God is not supernatural but "supertechnological"—that is, not almighty but a bit more mighty than us. Flying saucers were his agents in giving the world the Christian religion.

God is thus hoaxing us. He is a sort of technological magician, impressing us primitives with his scientific parlor-tricks so that we will worship him. He is incurably vain ("Anyone who doubts that God is a braggart has never read the Bible"[6]), not to mention irrational, pompous, easily angered and bored (the Christian religion is a devious game he is playing with humanity in order to alleviate his cosmic boredom). He deliberately misleads us in order to conceal the fact that his "omnipotence" is just technological hocus-pocus.

Given this kind of God, maybe the best argument against Dione's theory is that Dione hasn't yet been struck down by a thunderbolt! At last the gaff is blown—God's age-old camouflage is penetrated, his secret openly declared—and yet this irritable deity does nothing about it?

The Bible and Von Däniken Will Not Agree

From this account, it will be seen that Dione's theory is about the silliest I have read. It is a graphic demonstration of the absurdities one is involved in by trying to put von Däniken and the Bible together. The two just will not agree!

His argument is trivial and wrong. Apart from the usual crop of factual errors—there are not "hundreds" of miracles in the Bible, Job certainly did not come after Ezekiel, the Bible clearly talks about the Holy Spirit as a *person*—he treats the Fatima visions [7] as equally important with the New Testament (when even those statements of the "visitants" which he quotes contradict the New Testament) and uses the oddest arguments to justify his case:

"Finally, with the following question, I direct one last fatal blow at the authenticity of Jesus' power as a supernatural healer. Why did he not, with one all-inclusive announcement, heal all the faithful afflicted of his time? There is no reasonable answer to this question except the admission that indeed he was not supernatural'' (pages 108-9).

It never occurs to him that perhaps Jesus had a more important mission on earth than to heal all the "faithful afflicted." That if this *had* been his mission, we would have had to ask why Almighty God let them get sick in the first place. Or that if he had healed them all, with a wave of his hand, the one nationwide event wouldn't have drawn to him the questioning attention which smaller, more personal miracles did.

Reasonable Minds Can't Possibly Believe in Miracles— Or Can They?

Like Barry Downing, Dione assumes both that no scientific mind could possibly believe in miracles, and that the Bible account of things is to be judged by its probability. But in addition he makes incredible assumptions of his own.

The most outstanding is his view of what miracles are. "The church definition differs from the dictionary definition on two major points: According to the church, miracles are God's tools and no laws of nature can account for them, whereas, according to the dictionary, miracles are not necessarily God's acts and may be explainable by natural laws as yet unknown'' (page 43).

This is simply not so. No reasonable Christian would deny that miracles may obey "laws of nature"—they're mysterious only because we haven't yet discovered the "laws of nature" they obey! To the Christian, the hand of God can be seen in all his works, whether they can be "understood" or not; says scientist David Siemens, "One kind of explanation does not necessarily exclude another kind of explanation"[8] —that is, even if you have a "scientific" explanation for a happening (this airplane is flying because of aerodynamic principles) you haven't exhausted the possibility of *other* types of explanation (this airplane is flying because the pilot's mother is very sick a hundred miles away).

And so even if Dione found a "scientific" explanation for all the miracles of the Bible (which he certainly hasn't), he would not have explained away the Christian faith. As it is, some of his explanations (a cloud-camouflaged UFO feeding the 5000?) demand more credulity than any miracle in the Bible. Mary artificially inseminated under hypnosis by hypodermic syringe.... The soldier at the cross telepathically compelled to drive his spear into Jesus' side, by a UFO hovering overhead.... After a while we grow tired of seeing reds under the bed, or rather spacemen in the basement.

The theories we have examined so far are only theories. The average man buys a book on ancient astronaut theories, reads it through with a sort of vicarious thrill at the new possibilities it suggests, and then throws it away, saying, "Well, it could be." But the new gospel according to science fiction has also been taken seriously as the basis for "up-to-date" religious belief.

Notes to Chapter II

1. B.H. Downing, *The Bible and Flying Saucers* (1973), page 6.
2. W. Raymond Drake, *Gods and Spacemen in the Ancient East* (1973), page 68.
3. B.H. Downing, *The Bible and Flying Saucers* (1973), page 161.
4. Which we don't, incidentally. See John 20:26-9.
5. M. Jeeves, *The Scientific Enterprise and the Christian Faith* (1969), page 33.
6. R.L. Dione, *God Drives a Flying Saucer* (1973), page 123.
7. Alleged appearances of the Virgin Mary to children at Fatima in 1917.
8. D. Siemens, *Exploring Christianity* (Chicago, 1962), page 38n.

CHAPTER III
OUTER-SPACE
RELIGION

CHAPTER III

OUTER-SPACE RELIGION

Late in the 1940s, according to Dr. Chiistopher Evans, a group of science fiction writers met together to discuss the weakness of orthodox religions. They started to sketch out the features that a successful modern religion would need to have. It would need to draw its philosophy from science fiction, they decided, and its technique from psychoanalysis. . . .

The Church of Scientology
One of that group was a well-known science fiction author named L. Ron Hubbard. Now, just over 20 years later, he is the director and prophet of one of the fastest-growing of modern religions, with an annual income running into millions of dollars: The Church of Scientology, of California.

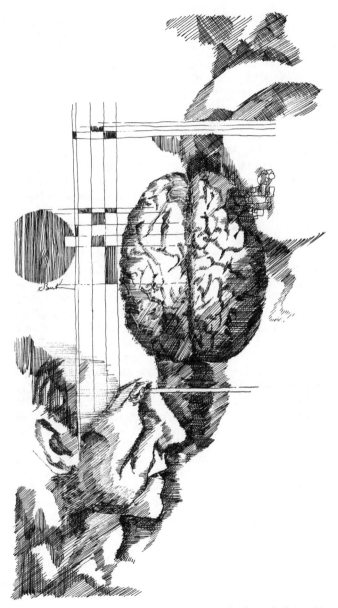

His new religion came to prominence thanks to the science fiction magazine, *Astounding Science Fiction*. The editor, John Campbell, was a close friend of Hubbard's and when his off beat ideas about psycho-therapy helped Campbell recover from sinusitis, he gave Hubbard space in the magazine for an article on "Dianetics" (as Hubbard named his new system). Within weeks, the Dianetics fad swept America; Hubbard toured the country lecturing, and his book *Dianetics: The Modern Science of Mental Health* was a best-seller almost as soon as it appeared. Dianetics was just a "technology," just a new method of psycho-therapy. Eventually Hubbard evolved a philosophy to go alongside it (from Buddhism, mainly) and called the result Scientology.

There has always been a bit of a gap between the technology and the philosophy. The Church of Scien-tology itself recognizes that the two things can be separated: "The philosophy lays down the creeds and codes of the church....The technology is the applica-tion of these findings to the individual...." Some Scientologists seem more interested in the technology than the philosophy; Maurice Burrell was told by an ex-Scientologist "that he was interested in the process of Scientology because he thought there was something factual in them, but that he had no time at all for Hubbard's philosophy."[1] And Cyril Vosper, another ex-member, exclaims:

"On one hand Hubbard offers undoubted benefits in terms of increased awareness, mental calmness, a point to an otherwise often pointless existence. On the other, he demands strict adherence to an extraordinary set of beliefs, pseudoscience, opinions and folk-lore."[2]

The technology of Scientology does work. It has made a lot of people better balanced mentally, has enhanced their ability to cope with life. Vosper, despite his

extreme disillusionment with the movement, still believes that "the discoveries of Scientology...are equally valid and probably superior to any other in psycho-
therapy."

Perhaps, though, it works because it isn't *too* far
removed from the procedures of mainstream psycho-
therapy. Burrell certainly thinks so: "What he seems to
have done is to take up some of the ideas of psycho-
logists, to have dressed up these ideas in certain
'Hubbardisms' like 'analytical mind,' 'reactive mind,'
'engram' and 'anaten,' to have combined these with
ideas from various other sources, and to have put
forward the whole conglomeration as first Dianetics and
then later Scientology" (page 28).

Learn the Meaning of Life by Studying Outer Space

But what interests me more, for our present purposes, is the incredible ramshackle structure of "philosophy" which has been built on to the limited success
of his psychotherapeutic ideas. It's another manifesta-
tion of the same principle that we saw at work in von
Däniken: finding the meaning of life by discussing
outer space; establishing a truly modern religion on the
basis of ray guns and Galactic Federations, rather than
less "modern," "scientific," theological concepts.

According to Hubbard, you and I consist of a body
inhabited by a Thetan, a spiritual entity which has "no
mass, no wave-length, no energy, no time or location in
space except by consideration or postulate." [3] The
Thetan is immortal and we all created, or helped to
create, the universe. We had fantastic powers, which
we have lost since, and which we can begin to regain
through Scientology. And so Hubbard feels the need to
counsel his followers not to show off their powers by
knocking off hats at 50 yards or reading books a couple
of countries away.

How long we have been around is uncertain. Hubbard's *History of Man* claims at different points that it's been 60, 70 and 76 trillion years, but we have all had numerous past lives. Under therapy details of these past lives come out: "Scientologists have been Galactic Emperors, doll-body slave drivers, ray-gunners and captains of Z-velocity space cruisers that save the Planet of the Beautiful Maidens from the Super Nova." [4]

Obviously, the population explosion suggests problems for this scheme: if all bodies are inhabited by Thetans, there must be a lot more Thetans around than there used to be. And indeed, this is the case: new Thetans are being dumped on earth, dropped into oceans (packed in "Ice Cubes") by flying saucers. Why? Well, the Galactic Federation is torn apart by wars, and political prisoners are being shipped here so as to get rid of them. This also explains the amount of political unrest on this planet today.

The written history of the world is deliberate lying. Historians have falsified the details because the truth would be too nightmarish. Von Däniken thinks people are scared of the truth. Hubbard thinks it would drive them mad. Only 2,000 years ago, for example, we were visited by the Fifth Invaders—space beings like insects, with horrible mandibles and claws, but six feet tall. They scared us so much that the human race has felt a revulsion from spiders and insects ever since.

Psychotherapy and Religious Mythology

And so we could go on. Vosper ironically sums it up: "The Past Track appears full of simple-minded Baddies giving the even simpler-minded Goodies a going over with various electronic devices. Hubbard has not even bothered to make his ramblings seem believable..." (page 66). But it is significant, I would argue, that a man who has constructed a religious mythology around a psychotherapy system, in the 20th century, hasn't had recourse to the traditional imagery—heaven and hell, good spirits and bad—but to the mythology of science fiction. Hubbard is the most extreme example of the *Gospel According to Science Fiction* turned into a religion.

The Thinking Man's Von Daniken

John Michell could be described as "the thinking man's von Daniken." His books are just as revolutionary, but far more scholarly, much less arrogant. The thinking is clearer, the argument more stringent. Thus it's not surprising that Michell—by all accounts a shy, retiring, scholarly figure—has attracted a large following among more intelligent young people with mystical inclinations.

For a short while he was idolized by the Underground, as a Messiah of a new expanded consciousness, and the ideas of his books influenced albums by several rock groups, including reputedly the Rolling Stones. Certainly his theories led to the massive hippy invasion of Glastonbury. *Time Out* hailed him as "a genius ... short-circuiting established channels of thought and offering a brilliant network of his own."

Michell's main plea—the one that intrigued mystical hippydom—is for a massive expansion of human consciousness. "Although every form of human development is limited to that which we can conceive of attaining, there is no reason to doubt that our potential is capable of a sudden, marked expansion."[5] This will come by a return to hidden wisdom known to our more "primitive" forefathers—who understood the mystical science of numbers, who were instructed by astronauts. "Given one more key, another inspiration from outside, we may be capable of an expansion of consciousness comparable to that achieved as on the first occasion when we were visited by people from space" (page 35).

His first book, *The Flying Saucer Vision,* describes this first visit. The proof of it is in "the earliest myths," which describe a meeting between men and an extra-terrestrial race, a meeting which produced "a revolutionary change in the whole pattern of human existence. This is the literal message of mythology..." (page 20). Is it?

Myths Tell Us When Astronaut Gods Appeared

He believes in "comparative mythology"—putting all the myths of the nations together and extracting *only their common features*. The trouble with this, unfortunately, is that you tend to end up with a compromise account which is quite unlike any of the myths you started with! When the gods came to earth, in his version, "At first it seems, their coming caused misery and chaos. Men became aware of things which before had been entirely inconceivable. From their primal state of innocence they became committed to the task of developing their newly-realized potential to the full.... Not unnaturally men looked back to the former times with a hopeless yearning for the golden age now irretrievably lost" (page 21).

Would you recognize that Adam and Eve had gone into the making of that story? Further, "In the period immediately preceding the arrival of the gods, men became aware of certain peculiar signs and portents in the sky" (page 21). It's not difficult to think offhand of six or seven cultures which believed otherwise.

In his eagerness to press stories into his service, he can ignore their obvious meaning. His humorless approach to the Wise Men of Gotham is one example. He refers to their plan to build walls to keep the cuckoo in Britain so that summer would last forever; incredibly enough, "the walls...turn out to be those earthworks with which so many prehistoric sacred places were surrounded and which were later used as fortresses. The cuckoo, a bird of ominous reputation...is a fitting symbol for the visitors from the sky" (page 156).

It's hard to see why the earthmen should have been so keen for these astronauts to stay, considering that a page or two before he had been identifying them with the evil Worm of Linton that devastated the countryside.

"Comparative Mythology" Is Dangerous

"Comparative mythology" involves a lot of dangerous assumptions. For example, that *every* nation on earth would make the imaginative connection between (long, thin) serpents and (round) flying saucers, and use the one to symbolize the other. Or—more important —that the only features of a myth which are of any use are *those which are shared with myths from somewhere else*. You rule out of court, before you even start arguing, the possibility that one set of myths might be closer to the truth than the others! And you assume that there's more similarity between myths than in fact there is:

"In some myths a creator exists before all things and may simply create the earth; or the world may arise from parts of the creator's body. In the widely diffused myth of the world-parents the sky father descends upon the earth mother and begets the world, or the sky and earth are joined and must be separated to permit life on earth.... Specific myths deal with man's arrival on earth; for example, he may descend from the sky or (in a myth common to aboriginal North and South America) he may emerge from under the ground."[6]

Hence when Michell claims that the myths give a "true reflection of historical events at the dawn of human civilization" (page 139) we're forced to ask, "*Which* myths? They can't all be right."

Michell has to regard anything in a myth that doesn't fit his scheme as a later accretion. Thus he can use the story of Hercules and the dragon as evidence of his theory (that dragons=spacecraft) *provided* he dismisses details such as the dragon's parentage, the reputed origin of the tree, the fact that different accounts exist of how exactly Hercules cheated the dragon. But who is to say what is the real core of the myth, and what is irrelevant addition? Michell quotes with approval Soviet scientist Agrest's "message to the Russian people ...that myths and legends from the past should be re-examined without reference to their later religions and scholarly accretions." But who decides what came first, and what was added?

Beowulf and the Flying Saucer

Let us take just one example. The story of Beowulf's fight with the dragon—says Michell—really celebrates the encounter of *homo sapiens* and the flying saucer. If this is so, what does he make of Beowulf's contests earlier in the poem, with a monster called Grendel, and then with Grendel's mother? Some scholars maintain that Beowulf's dragon-fight is just a rattling good story; others believe it to be an allegory of Christ in Gethsemane. Says Klaeber, the greatest of Beowulf scholars, "Grendel has figured as the incarnation of the terrors of pestilential marshes, malaria or fog, or of the long winter nights, a storm being....Also the dragon and Beowulf's dragon fight have been subjected to various interpretations of a similar allegorizing character." [7] Is it fair of Michell to assume blandly—without argument—that *his* interpretation is right, and everyone else's is wrong?

There are more difficulties yet! The date of the poem is far from certain, but many scholars accept a fairly late date. There's a real possibility, then, that this version of the Beowulf story may be by someone who didn't really understand its original "meaning" (if it had one) and so distorted the myth. How do we know that a late Christian author, in reproducing a pagan myth, hasn't altered the most important part of the story without realizing?

Michell claims that men first of all worshipped the astronauts, then later their machines (this explains why some men worshipped serpents and some didn't—"the serpent, the vehicle of the gods, came to stand for the gods themselves"). Finally (to explain sun and moon worship) "a cult for these and other heavenly bodies did later arise to complement or supplement the original worship of the actual gods" (page 22). Which came first, the chicken or the egg? It's just as possible that primitive men worshipping natural forces came later to give them human attributes—progressing *from* sun-worship *to* gods made like men.

In *City of Revelation* he advances the startling theory that Gnosticism was the real belief of early Christians (including Paul, John, Luke), that the New Testament is cryptically written in terms of a mystical numerological language, and that "it was not until the second century, when the hard party men took control of the newly-organized church, that gnosticism became a heresy" (page 116). All one can say is that Michell can't have read the New Testament. The forthright denunciation of the gnostic claim in Colossians, I Corinthians, Jude, I John and several other books; the fact that John (on whom Michell leans so heavily) was obviously writing *against* Gnosticism theory in gnostic language; the skimpy proof he produces for his theory from only five or six texts—the whole idea is a complete travesty of Church history in order to follow out his preconceived ideas.

Facts Are Often Doctored
Facts often need to be "doctored" slightly to fit the theories. It's suspicious, for one thing, that in *Flying Saucer Vision* and *City of Revelation* he offers completly different accounts of the meaning and construction of Stonehenge. He attempts to link John's New Jerusalem in the Book of Revelation with Glastonbury and Stonehenge, as the ideal plan for a temple. That

ignores several facts (the New Jerusalem *isn't* a temple, and has no need of one—Revelation 21; there is a perfectly good non-Cabbalistic explanation of the New Jerusalem's dimensions; some details of the city are obviously inserted because they are the *reverse* of pagan astrology; Solomon's temple and Ezekiel's don't fit his pattern) and juggles several others.

For a start, his reconstruction of the New Jerusalem (obviously worked out with one eye on Stonehenge) doesn't agree with anyone else's that I know of. Michell assumes that John is trying to describe a squared circle, but there are more obvious ways of reading the text! For one thing, his assumptions mean that he can't use the actual measurements given in Revelation. So he changes them to "commensurable proportions," and then argues from his new figures! To make numbers mean what he wants them to mean, he has to assume that John thought in terms of two different measuring systems at the same time—cubits and feet—and that the Stonehenge builders did too. One important figure in his Stonehenge calculations—79.2 feet—is only a "reasonable estimate"; in fact, if he's guessed slightly wrong and it's 79.1 or 79.3, his whole calculation falls to the ground.

Given this amount of flexibility, it's not difficult to make figures mean anything. And the annoying thing about John Michell is that he never considers an alternative theory. When one counts up, at the end of *Flying Saucer Vision*, what he's actually proved, there seems to be nothing that's incapable of a different interpretation. Men have always been fascinated with the possibility of flight?—Yes, ever since they watched birds. There's been a tradition of sexual acts with alien people from the skies?—Yes, but there have also been traditions of mermaids, silkies, Sirens... all, most likely, mythological evocations of the very human problem of the unattainable loved one. And so on. Michell really demands more respect and attention than I have given him here, because he *is* a clearer thinker than von Däniken; but the way he uses his knowledge, selecting facts and distorting history to substantiate an unprovable hypothesis, is not very reasonable at all.

Notes to Chapter III

1. M. Burell, *Scientology* (1970), page 10.
2. C. Vosper, *The Mind Benders* (1973), pages 20-21.
3. Scientology Axiom One.
4. Vosper, page 69.
5. J. Michell, *Flying Saucer Vision* (1967), page 19.
6. Prof. Alan Dundes, *Primitive Mythology* in Encyclopedia Britannica 15 (1968), page 1141.
7. F. Klaeber, Introduction to his edition of *Beowulf* (Boston, 1950), page 25.

CHAPTER IV
EZEKIEL SAW
DE QUASI-CONICAL
SPACECRAFT. . .

CHAPTER IV

EZEKIEL SAW DE QUASI-CONICAL SPACECRAFT

Did Ezekiel See a Spacecraft?

When Cristoph Blumrich phoned home one evening and told his father about the fascinating book he'd been reading—entitled *Chariots of the Gods?*—the response was fairly sceptical. For J.F. Blumrich was a National Aeronautics Space Administration engineer, working on large rockets and spacecraft as chief of the systems layout branch. However, Christoph sent the book, and his father started to read. It all seemed fantastic. Then he read von Däniken's claim that the vision described by the prophet Ezekiel at the start of his prophecy was actually a report of a spacecraft. And Blumrich had the idea of proving von Däniken wrong by checking the biblical account—after all, he knew all about spacecraft.

Ezekiel Saw De Quasi-Conical Spacecraft . . . 81

"Hardly ever," he writes, "was the total defeat so rewarding, so fascinating, and so delightful."[1] Study of Ezekiel had convinced him that von Däniken was right, that the prophet *had* seen a spacecraft; and Blumrich then wrote *The Spaceships of Ezekiel* to explain why. "Startling proof," proclaim his publishers, "taken from the *Bible*!" Does Blumrich's work make von Däniken any more credible?

I don't believe it does; because Blumrich makes some frighteningly big assumptions, and fails to ask a lot of questions he should have asked. I have no space here to deal with his theory in full; but here are a few questions he might have asked himself.

Is Ezekiel's Account Unique?
1.   Is Ezekiel's account unique, or do other prophets write in a similar style?

If Ezekiel saw a spacecraft in Ezekiel 1, what about the visions in Isaiah 6 and Daniel 10—similar in style, but unlike spacecraft as Blumrich describes them? If Chapter 1 (the vision) is to be understood as a scientific description, what do you make of the dry bones that come to life in Chapter 37?—to pick only one example. If the man in clothes of linen is actually wearing a protective suit, what about the figure in Daniel 7, who is *certainly* not doing a repair job on a spacecraft? Could it be that Blumrich has simply misunderstood the figurative way a prophet talks?

Who Else Saw It?
2.   Wouldn't we expect somebody else to see the spacecraft?

The vision took place at Tel Abib—a refugee settlement closely packed on a mound left by storms on the banks of the river Chebar. It's hard to see how one man could have got enough solitude to be the *only* spectator

of the noisy landing! Not far away were the great Babylonian astronomy schools, with astrologers ceaselessly scanning the sky for portents. An event as noisy and bright as Ezekiel suggests would have been visible over much of Babylon.

There are other improbabilities. He has to posit a *second* spacecraft on Chapter 11—but Ezekiel would surely have mentioned it, at least. He never explains how on earth the spaceship got inside Ezekiel's house in 8:1—quite a feat of navigation!

Is This Type Spacecraft Possible?
3.   Is it certain that this type of spacecraft is possible?

Blumrich isn't describing a type of spacecraft we can build now; he has to assume that we will one day find out how to make this sort of thing fly! "The actual principle of the central power plant," he has to admit, "cannot be closely defined" (page 30).

What's What?
4.   How do I tell what's "figurative" from what's "realistic," and what's "technical description" from what's "religious interpretation"?

As long as Blumrich believes he can keep the scientific details "clearly distinct from the prophetic content," he can't lose! Any fact that doesn't fit his theory can be dismissed as "figurative"...anything the astronauts say, that doesn't suit his interpretation of their actions, is just "religious interpretation."

Is It Proved?
5.   If a thing is possible, does that mean it's proved?

On page 69, for example, he claims that Ezekiel spoke of a "throne" in his vision because that's what a space machine's pilot seat looks like. Possible...but then he goes on cheerfully, "The word 'throne' thus clearly defines the seat of the commander" (page 69). This sort of jump, from "it could be" to "it is," weakens the argument time and again.

Are There Other Explanations?
6. Are there alternative explanations for mysterious points?

He has to ignore the fact that the meaning of Ezekiel's vision is not really mysterious, but has a perfectly good explanation without resort to flying saucers. Blumrich is determined to see mystery everywhere—Ezekiel, he says, could not have been transported to Solomon's temple in his visions, because he talks about an "outer court" and an "inner court," whereas Solomon's had only one court. The implication is obviously that Ezekiel was taken off to another planet. Until, that is, you take the trouble to look at a map of Soloman's temple, which included an outer court, middle court *and* inner court.

Who Wrote What?
7. What did Ezekiel write, and what isn't genuine?

On virtually no proof (can you really settle the authorship question of Ezekiel by a quick look at two commentaries as does von Däniken?) he assumes that Ezekiel doesn't really say what Blumrich wants him to say because the whole thing has been revised by a later editor. Now there were extensive attempts earlier this century to split different bits of Ezekiel up into "original ms." and "editor's gloss," but unfortunately no two scholars could agree on which bits belonged to whom! Nowadays most scholars follow C.G. Howie in believing that the traditional view—"Ezekiel wrote it"—is much more convincing. [2] The book is so homogenous, anyway, that if it was edited by anybody, Ezekiel himself may have been the editor!

What Other Reading Is Possible?
8. Is my reading of the text of Ezekiel the only one possible?

He assumes, from comparing six translations, that he is qualified to pronounce definitively on what every single word means. In fact, as the *New Bible Dictionary* points out, "Many hapax legomena[3] and technical expressions and obscurity in the symbolical language have led scribes into frequent error."[4]

Are the Facts Factual?
9. Does my explanation cover all the facts, without omission, distortion, or addition?

Occasionally he is stumped—"For the time being there is no satisfactory explanation for the light effect" (page 95)—but more often he ignores ill-fitting facts. The "space crew" are ordered to destroy the inhabitants of the city in 9:5—rather alarming, if this is a literal account, not a vision!—and what explanation does Blumrich offer? "Verse 5: the other men also receive assignments" (page 80).

Again, he has to twist the text at several points to fit it to his scheme. "Verse 24 and also verse 25 do not really belong here, because they describe the still-running motors...." "The statement is merely a fragment...a remainder of an originally longer passage." "This verse appears too early in the text. To be consistent with the course of events, it would belong to verse 6" (see pages 82, 107, 111). If you can fling verses around in this cavalier fashion, you can make them mean anything.

Blumrich has not really succeeded in backing up von Däniken with solid proof. Instead, he has painfully demonstrated how much you have to distort if you're really going to follow through the implications of the astronaut theory!

The Same "Mysteries," Different Conclusions

The phenomenal success of von Däniken has, not surprisingly, brought about a rash of like-minded books. We shall not have time to discuss all of them, and I think it would be pointless anyway. One suspicious thing is that they all trundle out the same few "mysterious" details—Stonehenge, the Great Pyramid, Piri Re'is, Tiahuanaco, Easter Island—and yet each one, arguing with the same facts, arrives at a slightly different conclusion. Charles Berlitz, for example, declares:

"...when, from a point of view so far back in time that we usually label it a marker of emerging civilization, we find uniquely exact descriptions of the effects of our most modern weapons, we wonder whether history is a repetition of vast concentric circles...." [5]

Well—to name but one—von Däniken doesn't.

Perhaps, though, we should look briefly at some writers who have tried to improve on von Daniken, from one point of view or another. Have they, in fact, succeeded in making his ideas more believable? Or have they just highlighted yet more contradictions and difficulties?

Notes to Chapter IV

1. Josef Blumrich, *The Spaceships of Ezekiel* (1974), Foreword.
2. C.G. Howie, *The Date and Composition of Ezekiel* (1950).
3. Word of which only one use is recorded.
4. Page 407.
5. C. Berlitz, *Mysteries from Forgotten Worlds* (1972), page 219.

CHAPTER V

HOW TO SELL
25 MILLION COPIES

CHAPTER V

HOW TO SELL 25 MILLION COPIES

Why the Interest in Astronaut Gods?
Twenty-five million copies is a lot of books. How are we to account for this phenomenon—this sudden burst of public interest in weird theories that would rewrite history completely, theories replete with flying saucers and ray-guns and extra-terrestrial visitors? Why are so many people keen to reconcile science and the occult? How have Erich von Däniken and L. Ron Hubbard achieved the attention they enjoy?

Common Features of the Theories
To answer these questions, I think we have to analyze a few of the typical features of the theories we have dealt with. All of them, I would say, have at least five traits in common.

SCIENTIFIC

"It should be much easier," protests Dione, "for anyone to picture a UFO removing the slab from the tomb than to imagine an invisible, supernatural being shouldering it out of the way." [1] Dione, and the others, continually appeal to our "scientific" expectations. There's a feeling that scientific knowledge, tested, tried and experimented upon, is somehow more trustworthy than any other kind of "knowledge."

This is why von Däniken, for all his scorn of experts, is forever quoting their names to impress us and support his argument! "What does Professor D.L. Pieper of Stanford University say?" he cries. And, "The systems analyst Jay W. Forester of the Massachusetts Institute of Technology has made an extremely detailed study...." If you support him, apparently, your full initials are given; but opponents are lucky to have their surname mentioned.

Louis Pauwels and Jacques Bergier (probably the direct source of most of von Däniken's ideas) are just the same. "One fine afternoon in June, 1963, I sat in the club library having tea with the nephew of one of these two men who had founded a religion...." [2]

The wilder one's theories, the more important to give them "scientific" credibility. Perhaps one reason for von Däniken's supremacy over his rivals is that he hasn't indulged in the creation of private occult philosophies—unlike (say) Drake and le Poer Trench.

"Old religions fade.... The decline of Christianity is marked by modern cynicism about a Hell where one burns for an eternity." So say the Scientologists. But in their religion, "the superstition has been subtracted from spiritual studies."

All of our theorists are trading on the growing public belief that the traditional religions are "unscientific" and that a new kind of religion must be found which is cleaner, more technical, more practical. There is a growing public hunger for something to believe in—something which combines the certainties of science with a religious optimism about our future that science on its own wouldn't justify.

ESOTERIC

Alvin Toffler states, "Today the hammerblows of the super-industrial revolution are literally splintering the society. We are multiplying...social enclaves, tribes and mini-cults among us almost as fast as we are multiplying automotive options. The same destandardizing forces that make for greater individual choice with respect to products and cultural wares, are also destandardizing our social structures. This is why, seemingly overnight, new subcults like the hippies burst into being. We are, in fact, living through a 'subcult explosion.' " [3]

Part of the appeal of our theorists stems from the fact that they offer a new "subcult." In a rapidly changing society, where the old answers no longer seem to fit the new problems, people are struggling to find a new framework of meaning within which to build their lives. And they tend to reject out of hand the possibility that the answers they're looking for may still be found in the most obvious places. Mysticism, meditation, Hindu subcults, drug experiences...we *expect*, nowadays, to find truth in these areas. At any rate there is security, and a feeling of superiority to the rest of the world, who Don't Belong. Trying to explain the phenomenal rise of the Divine Light Mission, Richard Levine comments, "Most of all there is the creation of a sense of community at a time of disintegrating social structures."

The books we have analyzed all stress that they are for The Few. "It took courage to write this book, and it will take courage to read it." So begins *Chariots of the Gods?* "If my theory is disproved," writes Paul Thomas (in *Flying Saucers Through the Ages*), "this will be a relief to many people!" And Louis Pauwels reflects that "this optimistic theory will bring a tired smile to many people's lips, for today a cynical doom-ridden attitude is the fashion."

We are living in crucially important days—if you are one of the Initiated, and can understand. Michell foresees an imminent cataclysmic change in civilization. "Man stands on the threshhold of a new, thrilling Cosmic Age challenging the stars," believes Raymond Drake. And Brinsley le Poer Trench acclaims "this age in which we are now privileged to be living, the Age of Aquarius—the Age of Space."

The kind of optimism that science won't allow is thus to be sought in esoteric points of view—not in the mainstream of human thought. Our writers are very scornful of "civilization." "Our culture wears blinkers," declares Pauwels and Bergier, "like all other cultures....The blinkers limit our vision" (page 9). Michell agrees. "Compulsory attendance at the education mill...encourages such totally false impressions of the past, that it becomes hardly possible to understand the present or to foresee the future." [4] Trench believes our education system falsifies reality: children are "literally split in two. They are given two basically contradictory forms of 'reality' and taught that they must live by both. 'Do unto others as you would be done by' and 'Do the other fellow before he does you.'" [5]

And so these theories are holding out to the 20th century man-in-the-street the possibility that he, yes he too can know what the universe is all about. Obviously society as a whole is confused. Church leaders, politicians, scholars speak with discordant voices. How nice it is to know that you are one of the Privileged Few who understand the human situation!

MIND-EXPANDING

Max Lerner, a professor at Brandeis University, believes that space exploration is "very much a part of our time." It reflects, he says, a modern "hunger for human connection"; we may be technically sophisticated, but despite it all, "we are still lonely and estranged." [6]

Increasing capabilities, oddly enough, have led to an increasing awareness of our limitations. We must lose the idea that we are "the lords of creation," claims von Däniken. And to Desmond Morris we are just The Naked Ape, "the sexiest primate alive." "We are, despite all our great technological advances, still very much a simply biological phenomenon. Despite our grandiose ideas and our lofty self-conceits, we are still

humble animals, subject to all the basic laws of animal behavior.'' Sooner or later we'll be extinct. "Many exciting species have become extinct in the past, and we are no exception'' (page 240).

Dr. Paul Ehrlich points out that 40% of the population of the undeveloped world is under fifteen. This will mean a massive baby boom in the next decade, which could be fatal to the human race, because we're running out of food as it is. Furthermore, we're playing "environmental roulette,'' which may destroy our ability to produce even as much food as we are producing at the moment.

Drake mourns our predicament: "Wisdom brings humility; in this tortured twentieth century which began in a golden age and now stumbles to suicide, men see no purpose to their lives and like the cynical pagans of the past eat, drink and make merry for tomorrow they die. The schizophrenic masochism, the mad rush to mass destruction, so manifest in national crime and international conflict are evidence of humanity racked with inner tensions and fear of the future'' (pages 15-16).

In a situation where experts seem to be preaching an uncompromisingly grim message, small wonder if people start to look *beyond* the methods of science for a ray of hope. Says Colin Wilson, recommending occult investigation, "Man must believe in realities outside his own smallness, outside the 'triviality of everyday-ness,' if he is to do anything worthwhile'' (page 36).

Intellect alone isn't enough. It was thinking that got us into this mess. And so modern man throws away his mind, all too often, and starts looking for new perspectives, new experiences...drugs, demonism, Dianetics, anything that will allow fresh possibilities in an increasingly claustrophobic universe. Facts are not too important provided the idea is compelling. "When I met von Däniken recently I asked him why he didn't accept the simplest explanation that fitted the facts. Why drag in the visitors from space? His answer staggered me. 'What the hell is a fact?' he said. 'The facts change every few years. Now we know space travel is possible, we must be prepared for new explanations.' " [7]

The idea that we needn't be rats in a scientific trap is one of the most appealing features of Flying Saucer theories. Says Trench, "The time will come in the not too distant future when mankind may be able to reach the stars. . . . They will then become like 'gods,' capable of manipulating matter and be above 'time and space' " (page 104). The Science Fiction Gospel holds out the dream of a future when once again—as in the heyday of the Industrial Revolution—we shall be on top of the brute facts of life, and no longer suffer them to be on top of us.

SIMPLIFYING
Suppose—says le Poer Trench—that the ultimate nuclear destruction were to happen tomorrow. Whom would men turn to for comfort? Not the nuclear physicists—but perhaps some roadside astrologer. "Among what is so contemptuously called the masses of humanity in our time, only the most fundamental of concepts has any possible chance of survival." [8]

The trouble with the nuclear physicists, and their kind, is that they have made life so complicated. Jaques Monod, a noted biolgist, claims that science has made man conscious of his "total isolation"—"Who, then, is to define crime? Who is to decide what is good and what is evil?" [9] The master of his own fate, man must hammer out ethical ideas for himself. He knows too much now to rely on "traditional systems."

He knows too much. . . . Says Gordon Rattray Taylor, "Whereas before we had to make do with what nature provided, now we can decide what we want; this may be called chemical control. Soon, in the coming century, we shall achieve biological control; the power to say how much life, of what sort, should exist where." [10]

As life daily grows more complicated, we adopt strategies to simplify it for ourselves. Alvin Toffler remarks that one way is to adopt a certain "life-style." "Deciding, whether consciously or not, to be 'like' William Buckley or Joan Baez. . .rescues us from the need to make millions of minute life-decisions. . . . By zeroing in on a particular life style we exclude a vast number of alternatives from further consideration" (page 286).

Thus there is an obvious attraction in theories which declare that basically there's quite a simple answer to the universe, that "really" the human race was created by astronauts, that "really" the Christian faith was the offspring of a mushroom-eating cult. When scientific expertise is daily becoming further and further estranged from the general knowledge of the man-in-the-street, anything which simplifies the issues becomes very welcome. Thus von Däniken appeals to his reader to judge, with his *own* common sense, with his *own* eyes: "You don't need years of scholarly training, you can be an auto-didact like me." And thus the impact of Christianity-was-a-mushroom myth (a theory popular a while back): "Mr. Allegro's book will make a vague and widespread impression to the effect that Christianity as we know it is eyewash, that as far as opinion on matters of Christian dogma goes, Jack is as good as his master. . . ." [11]

"Back to the lost knowledge of our primitive forefathers!" cry Michell, Trench, Underwood, Berlitz. It's a stirring rallying-cry in days when "scientific" knowledge is multiplying and diffusing and complicating itself with every passing week. It's stirring—because it *simplifies.*

UNDEMANDING

Religion used to be a communal affair. It brought people together...it celebrated their common humanity. It was a kind of sharing. Ritual dances knit together the primitive tribe, and strengthened each member's loyalty; the center of village life, in 19th century Wales, was the chapel; the one place in Scotland where the whole community met together was the Kirk.

But now, in our fragmented modern community, the reverse is true. Religion is increasingly seen as something personal, something that divides a man off from other men. Churchgoing — communal coming-together — is declining dramatically. Jehovah's Witnesses, calling on householders, are well used to receiving the response, "I've got my own religion, thank you." Previous centuries discussed religious issues for hours on end; we get embarrassed when the subject is brought up.

The whole trend of society is towards non-involvement. Increasingly we have "modular relationships" with other people; letting them fulfill a certain function for us, but refusing to become more deeply involved with them. "So long as the shoe salesman fulfills his rather limited service for us...we do not insist that he believe in our God, or that he be tidy at home, or share our political values." [12]

And so there are distinct attractions in a religion which doesn't demand that we go anywhere, do anything, or share in any way, so long as we just believe.

Von Däniken's message is ultimately religious. Anyone who doubts this need only read the last chapter of

Gold of the Gods. He has distinct teachings to propound about the nature of God, about our place in the universe, about "the whole human task." He offers religious consolations: claiming, for example, that with the "step into the universe we shall have to recognize that there are not two million gods, not twenty thousand sects or ten great religions, but only one." Dr. G.H. Stephens commented dryly, "Theologians in the Judaeo-Christian tradition have known this for two millenia." [13]

All you have to do to be saved is believe the theory. And then, what vistas of hope open out!—At last we realize that "the whole human task consists in colonizing the universe and that man's whole spiritual duty lies in perpetuating all his efforts and practical experience. Then the promise of the 'gods' of peace on earth and that the way to heaven is open can come true." [14]

It's hopelessly naive—we have already pointed out that contact with superior civilizations might be a bad thing, and Professor Garrett Hardin has proved that we won't solve our population problems by shipping off excess people to the stars. [15] In one year Americans could set aside enough capital to send one day's increase in world population off into space—if they accepted an 18% drop in their standard of living. But it's attractive, because it sounds optimistic, and it demands no action.

The Convenience of a Pop Religion

Richard Levine calls the Divine Light Mission "a form of pop religion...pop religion says the common values of a culture are the keys to the Kingdom. There can be no dark reaches of sin and retribution...nothing but an uncritical mirroring of a generation's best hopes about itself." [16] The Sacred Muchroom theory has similar appeal, says John King; it offers "the opportunity of a change of brand loyalty, from a religion that is tough, precise and demanding to a religion without rules, a religion without doctrine, a religion without God" (page 142). The appeal of the astronaut theories is exactly the same: the convenience of a pop religion.

Notes to Chapter V
1. R.L. Dione, *God Drives a Flying Saucer* (1973), page 123.
2. L. Pauwels and J. Bergier, *Eternal Man* (1972), page 17.
3. A. Toffler, *Future Shock* (1971), page 260.
4. J. Michell, *City of Revelation*, page 9.
5. Trench, *Operation Earth* (1969), page 97.
6. Quoted in B. Steiger and J. Whritenour, *Flying Saucers are Hostile*, page 159.
7. Peter Lewis, article cited.
8. Trench, *Temple of the Stars* (1962), page 11.
9. J. Monod, *Chance and Necessity* (1970), page 160.
10. G. Rattray Taylor, *The Biological Time Bomb* (1970), page 19.
11. J.C. King, *A Christian View of the Mushroom Myth* (1970), page 136.
12. A. Toffler, op cit, page 96.
13. Thiering and Castle, op cit, page 42.
14. *Chariots of the Gods?* pages 118-119.
15. In *Heredity, 50* (1959), pages 68-70.
16. R. Levine, "When the Lord of all the 'universe played Houston," *Rolling Stone*, March 14, 1974.

CHAPTER VI

SCIENCE FICTION GOSPELS AND THE FACTS

CHAPTER VI

SCIENCE FICTION GOSPELS AND THE FACTS

Two Important Questions
This book has been largely concerned with criticism.
That was inevitable, but before ending I want to try to
be more constructive. I think there are two important
questions which we still have to answer:

1. If von Däniken and the others are wrong, can we
find a better answer: is there a religious theory around
today that convincingly answers the needs of the 20th
century?

2. The flying saucer theories may be improbable, but
can we know *for certain* that they are wrong?

We should be able by now to build up an Identikit
picture of the ideal modern religion. "Scientific"—
well, it may not make the repetitive claims to scientific
accuracy that von Däniken does, but nothing in it must
offend what we know to be fact about the universe.

"Esoteric?" We can do without the snobbish in-group appeal of most radical theories, but clearly it must be something different from what the majority of the population believe, because most people are simply bewildered.

It must be "mind-expanding," too; it mustn't ignore the intellect so much that it becomes intellectually dishonest, but it must open up more possibilities in human life than scientific reasoning can on its own. It must make sense of all the different issues of life, and be "simplifying" without being naively reductionist.

And "undemanding"...?

Ah, there's the rub.

The Real Answer Is in the Inner Change

I believe that if we want to find a real answer to life, we won't do it simply by believing any one of half a dozen theories. We will only do it by experiencing a deep inner change; we will only do it by involving ourselves in a relationship with someone.

Let me explain.

Von Däniken paints an unforgettable picture of the contemporary Christian—a bewildered modern man, educated scientifically but brought up on fairy tales, trying to piece together a few puzzling documents to work out whether something supernatural really *did* happen in the Middle East 2,000 years ago. But the believer can't be too sure any more—and every time another scientific advance is made, he becomes even more bewildered. So von Däniken asks, "Doesn't my theory sound more probable than yours?"

Now this is a total travesty. If all Christians had were a few documents to puzzle over, a few facts to juggle

with, then Christian belief wouldn't be an act of faith—
it would be a demonstration of lunatic dishonesty.
Certainly, if Christianity were to be judged simply by
probability, then perhaps even von Daniken's vagaries
would seem more "likely" than the wild claim that God
once came down here as a man. Although, when one
sets about trying to disprove the Christian claim, one
finds that there's an unexpectedly large heap of
evidence to dispose of—evidence for the resurrection,
for example, or for the total character-change of
believing people.

Our Willingness to Experience God Directly

But the Bible doesn't appeal to our sense of
probability. It appeals instead to *our willingness to
experience God directly!* The message underscoring
the whole of the New Testament is that human beings,
here and now, can know the friendship of God for
themselves. "Agree with God," cries the oldest book in
the Bible, "and be at peace!"[1] Down through the
centuries, millions and millions of people have been
convinced of the existence of God, not because they
read a book about Him—not because they were brought
up that way—but because they KNEW HIM for
themselves!

How does this happen?

When a radio set stops receiving messages we say it
has "gone dead." And according to the New Testament
each of us is "dead in trespasses and sins"—incapable,
that is, of receiving communications from God, because
of the imperfections and selfishness in our life that
"jam the transmissions" of a totally perfect God. To
bring us to life again, those imperfections have to be
dealt with.

Enter Jesus

Which is where Jesus comes in. "He who knew no sin was made sin for us, so that we could be accredited the perfect holiness of God in him."[2] By an act of incredible generosity, Jesus died willingly to pay the penalty which really we deserved to pay, for breaking God's laws. According to the Bible (and quite frankly I know it's true, from my own experience) this makes it possible for us to get to know God again, by simply inviting him to take command of our lives. Von Däniken believes that one day we will contact beings in another dimension. The Bible claims you can do it right now!

And ultimately, although it's effective to argue about Maya mythology and the Genesis Apocryphon and the Nazca markings, I do not distrust von Däniken and the others because the details of their argument are mistaken. I distrust them because I can't do anything else.

The God Who Created Everything, Lives!

If I know that the God who created everything is not only alive but also at work in my life right now, it becomes pointless for me to speculate that he may have been a bunch of spacemen. If you want to be certain sure whether the science fiction gospels tell the truth or not, there is only one thing to do: contact personally the great Reality who made the universe, and find out that even today he still keeps his promises. Then, and only then, you will have the answer. Living inside!

Notes to Chapter VI
1.   Job 22:21, RSV.
2.   2 Corinthians 5:21, RSV.